The Oregon Trail

R. Conrad Stein

CHILDREN'S PRESS
A Division of Grolier Publishing
Sherman Turnpike
Danbury, Connecticut 06816

Library of Congress Cataloging-in-Publication Data

Stein, R. Conrad.
  The Oregon Trail / by R. Conrad Stein.
    p. cm. – (Cornerstones of freedom)
  ISBN 0-516-06674-9
  1. Oregon trail–Juvenile literature. [1. Oregon Trail.
2. Overland journeys to the Pacific. 3. West (U.S.)–
History. 4. Frontier and pioneer life.] I. Title. II. Series.
F597.S8   1994
978–dc20
                         93-36994
                            CIP
                            AC

The mountain men said it was impossible for women and wagons to journey over the Oregon Trail. Travelers to the Oregon Country had to deal with Indians who might be hostile. They had to follow mountain paths difficult enough for a lone man and a mule. Women and wagons on that rugged trail? Never, said the mountain men.

Yet in the spring of 1836, a group of determined missionaries led by Dr. Marcus Whitman left the frontier town of Liberty, Missouri, and marched west. With the party were two missionary women and two wagons. Their destination was the Oregon Country, some two thousand miles away.

The first part of the trail was well established. Narcissa Whitman, wife of the leader, kept a diary of her trip. At first, she viewed her journey as a great adventure. But the endless flatlands of what are today Kansas and Nebraska soon left her a little bored. Her entry for June 3, 1836, reveals a monotonous routine: "Start usually at six, travel till eleven, encamp, rest and feed, start again about two, travel until six or before, then encamp for the night."

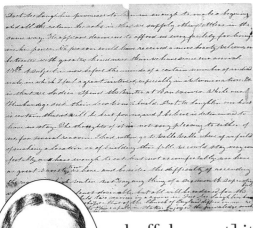

Narcissa Whitman kept a diary of her 1836 trek to the Oregon Country.

Weeks dragged into months as the terrain grew rugged. The missionaries' food supply dwindled. They lived on strips of dried buffalo meat. Along the Bear River in present-day Wyoming, Narcissa wrote, "I can scarce eat [the tough buffalo meat] it appears so filthy, but it will keep us alive and we ought to be thankful for it." Day after day, the unrelenting sun beat down on the party. On August 2, Narcissa wrote that it felt like walking inside a gigantic oven: "Truly I thought the heavens over us were brass, and the earth iron under our feet."

Still the animals pulled and the wagon wheels creaked. Soon the travelers saw the peaks of the Rocky Mountains towering ahead. Their dazzling beauty refreshed Narcissa. But crossing the majestic mountains was an ordeal. "Before noon we began to descend one of the most terrible mountains for steepness and length I have yet seen. It was like winding stairs in its descent and in some places almost perpendicular. The horses appeared to dread the hill as much as we did. They would turn and wind in a zigzag manner all the way down. We had no sooner gained the mountain when another more steep and dreadful one was upon us."

Crossing the Rocky Mountains was a tremendous ordeal for people traveling by horse or covered wagon.

On September 1, 1836, the exhausted and half-starved missionaries reached a fort built by fur traders near what is today the city of Walla Walla, Washington. Narcissa was overjoyed to see cabins and roads after so many miles of trackless wilderness. A rooster in the fort crowed and Narcissa wept with delight. "No one knows the feelings occasioned by seeing objects once familiar after long privation."

Narcissa Whitman and Eliza Spalding, the other woman in the party, were the first white women to cross the Rocky Mountains on the Oregon Trail. The wagons that Marcus Whitman had hoped to drag for the entire trip had to be abandoned on the eastern side of the mountains. Still, the Whitmans' success proved that farm families could endure the journey over the trail. The marvelous Oregon Country could now be opened for settlement.

Fort Walla Walla in the early 1800s

After arriving in the Oregon Country, the Whitmans established a mission near Fort Walla Walla.

At the time of the Whitmans' journey, the land commonly called the Oregon Country was a huge territory covering some 500,000 square miles. It included today's states of Washington and Oregon and stretched north almost to Alaska. Early in the 1800s, it was the home of Indian tribes and white fur trappers known as mountain men. At one time, both Russia and Spain had claims on the Oregon Country. But by the 1830s, only the United States and Great Britain haggled over ownership of the land.

Much of the Oregon Country was ideal for farming. But farming was a family affair, and the trip to Oregon was considered too hazardous for families. The only overland route to the area was the long and treacherous Oregon Trail.

Geography dictated the route of the trail. Most of it wound along the banks of three major rivers—first the Platte, then the Snake, and finally, the Columbia. The Oregon Trail existed long before explorers from Europe and America ventured into the Pacific Northwest. For hundreds of years, Indians had worn footpaths between mountains and along rivers. Later travelers on the two-thousand-mile route

Oregon Trail emigrants followed the North Platte River (top) from Nebraska into Wyoming. When they reached Independence Rock (bottom), their westward journey was about halfway over.

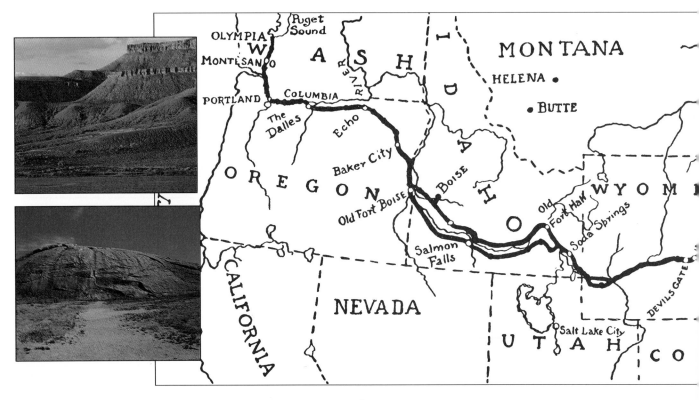

of the trail simply connected the hundreds of different Indian footpaths.

The first whites to travel parts of the trail were Meriwether Lewis and William Clark, who were sent by the American government to explore the Northwest in 1804. Although they took a more northerly route across the continent, they did travel along a section of the Oregon Trail in the region of the Snake and Columbia rivers. Lewis and Clark determined the immediate future of the Oregon Country when they wrote that the rivers and streams there teemed with beaver, otter, and other fur-bearing animals.

The 2,000-mile journey along the Oregon Trail took about six months to complete.

Trappers and fur traders followed almost on the heels of Lewis and Clark. Many of the trappers journeyed to the Northwest via the Oregon Trail. But some reached the country by ship. In 1811, representatives of John Jacob Astor's Pacific Fur Company arrived at the mouth of the Columbia River. They traveled inland twelve miles and established Astoria, a fur-trading post and the first permanent settlement in the Oregon Country. Later, the town of Astoria was considered the end of the Oregon Trail.

John Jacob Astor (left) began the white settlement of Oregon when his Pacific Fur Company established a fur-trading post there in 1811 (below).

Solitary trappers called mountain men used parts of the Oregon Trail years before pioneer families began flooding westward over the route.

During the 1820s and 1830s, the Oregon Trail was a major highway for the mountain men. They were a colorful lot. Their lives were filled with danger and contrasts. Mountain men both fought the Indians and lived with them. Many had Indian wives. They regarded the Oregon land as strange and hostile. Yet they forever plunged deeper into unknown territory in their search for fur-bearing animals. They chose their lonely and perilous way of life for several reasons. Some enjoyed the adventure. Other liked the money to be made in furs. Still others drifted into the Oregon Country to escape the law back East. A few mountain men—including Kit Carson, Henry Fraeb, James Bridger, and Tom Fitzpatrick—became legends of the Old West.

Kit Carson

James Bridger

11

When rumors of Oregon's fertile land and gentle climate began drifting back East, a wave of "Oregon fever" swept the United States.

Missionaries began entering the Oregon Country in the 1830s. The mountain men considered them to be "crazy do-gooders." But for a fee, the mountain men led the missionaries to remote Indian villages. The missionaries noted the fertile land and gentle climate of the Pacific Northwest. In letters home, they claimed that farms and ranches would thrive in the region. By the start of the 1840s, a wave of "Oregon fever" swept the United States. Hardy pioneer farmers dreamed of tilling the soil of a new frontier in Oregon.

For more than a hundred years, American farmers had pushed west seeking new and better land. The constant westward expansion led Americans to think of their nation as extending all the way to the Pacific. It hardly mattered that Mexico owned California and Texas or that Britain had claims on Oregon. The land to the west *had* to be theirs someday. They called their dreams for a nation that stretched from sea to sea the "Manifest Destiny" of the American people.

This 1861 painting glorifies the idea of Manifest Destiny–that the U.S. had a God-given right to settle the entire North American continent.

The United States government encouraged this attitude. In the East, politicians made fiery speeches claiming that the western half of the continent would soon become America's backyard. One New Jersey Democrat cried out, "Make way for the young American buffalo—he has not land enough. . . . I tell you we will give him Oregon for his summer shade and the region of Texas as his winter pasture. . . . The mighty Pacific and the turbulent Atlantic shall be his."

Thousands of settlers were stricken with Oregon fever. But a single question burned in their minds. Could they survive the perilous journey on the Oregon Trail?

In the long history of the American march westward, no wilderness passage was as difficult or as dangerous as the Oregon Trail. For wagons, the 2,000-mile trip would take six months. Only a few fur-trading outposts dotted the trail. Everything a farm family needed for the journey had to be jammed into its wagon. The trek over half a continent would carry pioneers over wildly varying landscapes. Travelers would find themselves sweltering in a desert one month, then shivering in a snowbank the next. They would have to ford rivers, struggle over back-breaking mountains, and drive through Indian country. They would suffer food shortages and would have to cope with dreaded diseases. And if they failed to

Because the journey over the Oregon Trail would be long and difficult, only the most useful and prized possessions were packed into a family's Conestoga wagon.

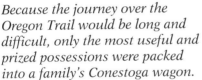

reach Oregon before winter, they might freeze to death in the mountains.

Despite these dangers, pioneer families chose to emigrate to the promised land called Oregon.

Fearful of Indian attacks, the early emigrants decided that large caravans of wagons would be the safest way to travel. The wagons chosen by the pioneers were sturdy Conestoga wagons used by Americans since the Revolutionary War. The Conestoga wagons were named after the Pennsylvania town where they were first built. Because they looked like ships with white sails, they were sometimes called "prairie schooners."

An 1860 wagon train stops in a Kansas town for a last purchase of supplies before the long trek across the plains.

Oxen were chosen to pull the wagons. They were slow but strong animals, and they could be used to pull plows once the farmers reached the Oregon Country.

The year 1843 marked the beginning of the mass movement of Americans to Oregon. In May of that year, the first of the great wagon trains left Independence, Missouri. It consisted of 1,000 men, women, and children, 120 wagons, and 5,000 assorted head of cattle. No one knows how many pigs, chickens, and hogs were taken along. Leading the parade of pioneers was a quiet but courageous Missouri farmer named Jesse Applegate.

Applegate wrote a lively account of a typical day in the lives of the people driving their wagons west over the Oregon Trail: "It is 4 A.M. The sentinels on duty have discharged their rifles—the signal that the hours of sleep are over." The emigrants barely had a chance to yawn before starting to work. Women built fires and hung over them pots of water to warm the morning coffee. At the time Applegate wrote his account, the wagons were crossing the Great Plains, where there was little firewood. Fires had to be made from dried buffalo dung, or "buffalo chips," as the settlers called them. The travelers usually ate a breakfast of sowbelly (bacon) and slam-Johns (flapjacks).

At seven each morning, Applegate gave the command, "Wagons ho!" Each wagon had to be in its assigned place at that time. The best positions were toward the front of the line. Those in the rear had to "eat dust" all day long.

Early in the morning, a sentinel on horseback signals that it is time to assemble the wagon train and begin a new day on the trail.

An Oregon Trail emigrant family

On Applegate's wagon train, families alternated places in line each day. Rarely was a wagon late assembling in the morning because "All know when, at 7 o'clock, the signal to march sounds that those not ready to take their proper places in the line of march must fall into the dusty rear for the day."

With cows mooing, dogs yelping, and wagon wheels creaking, the long caravan rolled toward Oregon. Applegate described how the "wagons form a line three quarters of a mile in length. Some of the teamsters [drivers] ride upon the front of their wagons, some walk beside their teams. Scattered along the line, companies of women and children are taking exercise on foot. They gather bouquets of rare and beautiful flowers that line the way."

A wagon train approaches Nebraska's Chimney Rock, a famous Oregon Trail landmark.

Plains Indians assisting Oregon Trail emigrants during a buffalo hunt

From far forward came the cry, "Buffalo! Buffalo!" About twenty young men riding horseback at the point of the column stormed after a small herd of buffalo. To the people in the wagon line, the riders and buffalo looked like specks on the horizon. Distant shots cracked. One sharp-eyed wagon driver called out, "They got one!" Some families would enjoy fresh meat that night.

At noon, the wagon train stopped for lunch— a hurried meal of dried meat. A few families sat at portable tables. Most ate standing up. During lunch, Applegate and a council of men served as judges in a traveling court. A young man who had agreed to work for a family in exchange for

A wagon train crossing the South Platte River in Nebraska

a bed and food complained that the head of the household was working him too hard. He did not even have time to take moonlit walks with his girlfriend. The judges heard arguments from the young man and his employer. They withheld an opinion until the next time the court met.

On the trail once more, the wagon train had to ford a river. Horsemen at the head of the column splashed about the stream seeking a rocky bottom that would be safe for the wagons. When a proper bed was found, a man marked it with a flag. The lead wagon plowed into the river. Water rose as high as the driver's feet, but the bottom was solid. Soon the whole train crossed the stream safely. Other rivers along the Oregon Trail would not be so easy.

It was almost dark when Applegate signaled a halt. The wagons formed a tight ring called a "night circle." This served as a barrier against Indian attack and also gave the camp a community atmosphere. Fires were lighted and the travelers enjoyed their largest meal of the day. Families ate buffalo or antelope steak or stewed prairie chicken. Wild game was often plentiful on the Great Plains. At other points along the Oregon Trail, the emigrants suffered through near-starvation diets.

As darkness crept over the camp, Applegate wrote, "Before a tent near the river a violin makes music, and some youths and maidens have improvised a dance upon the green. In another quarter a flute gives its mellow and melancholy notes to the still air." But the music ceased and fires were doused early. Morning would come soon, and the emigrants had to face another long day on the Oregon Trail.

A family takes a quiet meal along the trail.

The Oregon Trail led its travelers across terrain of dazzling variety.

The wagon trains averaged twelve to fifteen miles a day, depending on the terrain. And while crossing the western half of the continent, the emigrants saw terrain of dazzling variety.

At the trail's beginning, the endless flatlands of the Great Plains mystified settlers from the East. Trees grew only along the riverbanks, leaving the rest of the land a windswept sea of tall grass. About four hundred miles out of Independence, the travelers had to cross the treacherous south branch of the Platte River. They complained that the river was "a mile wide and six inches deep." Quicksand lined its banks, and the river bottom was a bed of ooze.

In present-day Wyoming, the travelers reached a fur-trading outpost called Fort Laramie. There they rested a few days and learned of the progress of the wagon train ahead of them. Following the banks of the Sweetwater River, the emigrants climbed into mountain country. At dizzying peaks, children were delighted to discover they could have snowball fights in the middle of August. A famous landmark of the trail was a turtle-shaped boulder called Independence Rock. Travelers dating back to the mountain men scratched their names on the face of the rock. Over the years, Independence Rock became known as the "register" of the Oregon Trail.

Fort Laramie in the 1800s (top) and today (bottom)

Wyoming's Sweetwater River Valley from the top of Independence Rock

While pushing over the mountains, the emigrants crossed the Continental Divide. Adults pointed out to children that west of this divide, the rivers along the trail flowed west to empty into the Pacific Ocean. East of the divide, they flowed east toward the Atlantic. The trail cut through South Pass. This was a gateway through the Rocky Mountains discovered in 1812 by a Scottish explorer named Robert Stuart. Next came the breathtaking Green Valley. Years earlier, the valley had been alive with beaver and otter, but those animals had been almost completely trapped out before the coming of the covered wagons. Children discovered that water from a stream called Soda Springs tickled their noses when they tried to drink. And the travelers agreed that the roaring of the rapids at Steamboat Springs really sounded like a Mississippi steamboat.

At the wilderness outpost at Fort Hall, in what is now Idaho, the Oregon Trail split. Those going to Oregon traveled northwest. Those heading for another promised land—California—drove southwest. The wild Snake River country next greeted the Oregon travelers. The exhausted people and animals had to struggle over their final mountain barrier—the rugged Blue Mountains. Finally, they arrived at Fort Walla Walla on the Columbia River. From there, most of the emigrants claimed land in the rich

Willamette Valley. Others took riverboats to the town of Astoria on the Pacific.

Emigrants had little time to celebrate their triumph upon reaching the Oregon Country. Winter was closing in by the time they arrived, and they had to fell trees and build cabins. The last page in the diary of one Oregon traveler ended:

> Friday, October 27. Arrived at Oregon City at the falls of the Willamette.
> Saturday, October 28. Went to work.

Before starting the long journey to Oregon, the emigrants had harbored three major fears— Indians, disease, and the weather.

Indians proved to be the least dangerous of

The emigrant's new homes had to be built quickly, before winter arrived.

their fears. As long as the emigrants kept moving, the Plains Indians allowed them to pass through their territory. Indian wars broke out primarily in areas where the whites began settling on Indian land. Contrary to what is seen in old movie westerns, massive Indian attacks on wagon trains were rare during the pioneering era. Indian bands that approached the trains did so to trade. Some Indians hired themselves out to travelers and helped them float their wagons over difficult rivers. Other Indians served as scouts for wagon trains and guided settlers through passages between mountains. But sometimes, Indians tried to steal the emigrants' cattle at night. For that reason, the settlers always posted

Encounters between Indians and Oregon Trail emigrants were usually peaceful.

Death from the disease cholera was probably the greatest threat to Oregon Trail travelers.

a night guard around their ring of wagons. Blood was sometimes spilled when Indian cattle rustlers clashed with night watchmen.

Rampant diseases killed many more Oregon travelers than did Indians. The most dreaded disease was an infection of the intestines called cholera. The disease was brought from Asia and swept the United States in the early 1800s. Extremely contagious, it jumped from one member of a wagon train to another. A person with cholera felt intense stomach pains and was seized by fits of vomiting. Death often occurred after twenty-four agonizing hours.

Those who died of cholera and other causes were buried alongside the trail. An emigrant named J. Goldsborough Bruff rode with a wagon train in 1849, and counted forty-five fresh graves in only three weeks of travel. It is estimated that during the pioneer years, 34,000 emigrants died

The grave of one of many pioneers who died along the trail

A wagon train caught in a snowstorm along the trail

and were buried along the trail. This dreadful
figure averages out to seventeen deaths for
each mile of the Oregon Trail.

The weather along the trail often meant
the difference between life and death for the
traveler. Frightening thunderstorms swept the
Great Plains during the summer. Farther west,
the trail cut through deserts where heat and
swarming flies made families curse the day
they had left their homes. The worst fate that
could befall a westward traveler was to be
trapped in the mountains during winter.

Still, the flow of emigrants to Oregon never
stopped. In 1843, Oregon's rich Willamette Valley
was an untouched wilderness. Two years later,
some five thousand American farmers were
busy tilling the soil there. All the new farmers
had arrived over the Oregon Trail.

The presence of so many American settlers gave the United States a great advantage in its clash with the British over ownership of the Oregon land. Americans argued that the land was theirs simply because they were already occupying it. So confident were the Americans that at one point they demanded an Oregon Territory whose borders extended north to what is now Alaska. "Fifty-four forty or fight!" became a popular slogan. The slogan referred to a 54°40' latitude line that many Americans believed should be the northern border of Oregon. In 1848, however, the United States and Great Britain agreed on a boundary line along the 49th parallel. That line remains America's northern border with Canada today.

After the treaty, the Oregon Trail remained a busy highway for emigrants. By 1850, the

By the late 1850s the Willamette Valley was filled with pioneers who had arrived over the Oregon Trail.

To this day, ruts left by thousands of wagon wheels can still be seen on parts of the trail.

register at Fort Laramie showed that 40,000 men, women, and children and 9,000 wagons had passed through the fort on their way west. Wagons continued to roll over the trail well after the transcontinental railroad was completed in 1869. As late as 1895, animal-drawn wagons still moved settlers over the Oregon Trail. On parts of the trail, ruts left by thousands of wagon wheels can be seen to this day.

The Oregon Trail opened the door to a new frontier, and the rugged American pioneers poured through. Author Henry David Thoreau described the westward urge of his countrymen best when he wrote, "Eastward I go only by force, but westward I go free. This is the

A monument honoring those who traveled the Oregon Trail

Emigrants Crossing the Plains, *an 1867 painting by Albert Bierstadt*

prevailing tendency of my countrymen. I must walk toward Oregon." By the end of the 1840s, America's manifest destiny had become a reality. The young nation stretched from sea to sea.

Travelers on the Oregon Trail found a rich land waiting. Many of them prospered and remained in the new country for the rest of their lives. But even after they grew old, the settlers would never forget their six-month, 2,000-mile journey over the plains, rivers, and mountains. It was a trek that had seen them laughing and crying, sweating and shivering, and storing up a lifetime of memories and dreams.

INDEX

PHOTO CREDITS

Cover, Benjamin Franklin Reinhart, *The Emigrant Train Bedding Down for the Night,* 1867, oil on canvas, 40 x 70 in. (101.6 x 177.8 cm), In the Collection of the Corcoran Gallery of Art, Gift of Mr. and Mrs. Landsell K.Christie; 1, Denver Public Library, Western History Department; 2, ©Tom Dietrich; 4 (top), Courtesy the Bancroft Library; 4 (bottom), Oregon Historical Society, neg.# OrHi 1645; 5, Stock Montage, Inc.; 6, Oregon Historical Society, neg.# OrHi 89932; 7, Scotts Bluff National Monument; 8 (top inset), ©Robert C. Clark; 8 (bottom inset), ©Mary A. Root/Root Resources; 8-9 (map), Stock Montage, Inc.; 10, (bottom), Oregon Historical Society, neg.# OrHi 21681; 10 (top), 11 (top), North Wind; 11 (middle), Courtesy Museum of New Mexico; 11 (bottom), The Kansas State Historical Society, Topeka, Kansas; 12 (top), ©Steve Terrill; 12 (bottom), Culver Pictures, Inc.; 13, National Museum of American Art, Washington, D.C./Art Resource, NY; 15 (wagon), ©Tom Dietrich; 15 (artifacts), Oregon Historical Society/©Harald Sund; 16, The Kansas State Historical Society/Topeka, Kansas; 17, Courtesy the Bancroft Library; 18 (top), Oregon Historical Society, neg.# OrHi 37784; 18 (bottom), Scotts Bluff National Monument; 19, Scotts Bluff National Monument; 20, Scotts Bluff National Monument; 21, The Kansas State Historical Society, Topeka, Kansas; 22 (top left), ©Larry Geddis; 22 (top right), ©Steve Terrill; 22 (bottom), ©Larry Schaefer/Root Resources; 23 (top), Scotts Bluff National Monument; 23 (middle), ©Littler/Fort Laramie National Historic Site; 23 (bottom), Denver Public Library, Western History Dept.; 25, Idaho State Historical Society; 26, The Thomas Gilcrease Institute of American History and Art, Tulsa, Oklahoma; 27 (top), Courtesy the Bancroft Library; 27 (bottom), ©Steve Terrill; 28, North Wind; 29, Oregon Historical Society, neg.# OrHi 21079; 30, ©Steve Terrill; 31, National Cowboy Hall of Fame and Western Heritage Center, Oklahoma City

Picture Identifications:
Cover: *Emigrant Train Bedding Down for the Night,* an 1867 painting by Benjamin Franklin Reinhart
Page 1: A group of Oregon Trail pioneers
Page 2: Some of the rugged Nebraska terrain crossed by Oregon Trail pioneers

Project Editor: Shari Joffe
Design: Beth Herman Design Associates
Photo Research: Jan Izzo

ABOUT THE AUTHOR

R. Conrad Stein was born and raised in Chicago. He enlisted in the Marine Corps at the age of eighteen and served for three years. He then attended the University of Illinois, where he received a B.A. in history. He later studied in Mexico, earning an advanced degree from the University of Guanajuato.

Mr. Stein is the author of many books, articles, and short stories from young people. He lives in Chicago with his wife and their daughter Janna.